EMOTIONAL INTELLIGENCE

Why Emotions Are Great Tools But Bad Bosses

Diane Weston

MONKEY
PUBLISHING

OUR HAND-PICKED
BOOK SELECTION FOR YOU.

LEARN
SOMETHING NEW
EVERYDAY.

Published by *Monkey Publishing*
Edited by *Lily Marlene Booth*
Cover Design by *Diogo Lango*
Printed by *Amazon*

1st Edition, published in 2019
2nd Edition, published in 2020
© 2020 by Monkey Publishing
Monkey Publishing
Lerchenstrasse 111
22767 Hamburg
Germany

ISBN: 9798575517887

TABLE OF CONTENTS

INTRODUCTION TO EMOTIONAL INTELLIGENCE......1

But I'm Just not Good with Feelings 1

Why We all Need to Improve our Emotional Intelligence
....3

RESEARCH ON EMOTIONAL INTELLIGENCE............5

But Does the Science Matter?...................................6

**THE THREE MODELS OF EMOTIONAL
INTELLIGENCE...9**

Ability Model 9

Mixed Model...11

Trait Model 12

**THE NECESSITY OF EI AND HOW YOU CAN IMPROVE
YOURS...13**

WHAT ARE EMOTIONS?..................................... 15

The Feeling Three 15

    The Feeling Three: Protection....................................15

    The Feeling Three: Just Passing Through 16

    The Feeling Three: Emotions are Great Tools but Bad
    Bosses 18

The Thinking Three: Thoughts, Habits, Perceptions 19

    How Thoughts Affect Emotions 19

    How Habits Affect Emotions 21

    Emotions Influence your World View 23

Emotion as a Tool is what Emotional Intelligence is all
About...24

LEARNING EMOTIONAL INTELLIGENCE..................26

The Four R's of Emotional Intelligence 26

The First R: Recognition...27

The Second R: Regulation 30

The Third R: Reading Signals 35

The Fourth R: Responding...40

DEVELOPING EMOTIONAL INTELLIGENCE.............45

How to Develop Recognition Skills 45

Noticing Feelings 45

Identify and Observe the Feeling 48

Identify Emotional Triggers 50

Evaluate the Appropriateness of Your Reactions..............52

How to Develop Regulating Skills...........................52

How to Use or Express Your Emotions 52

How to Change your Emotional State 58

How to Develop the Skills to Read Other People's
Signals.. 60

Eye Contact 61

Facial Expressions and Posture 62

Tone of Voice: Volume and Pitch..................................62

Reading Signals and Making Decisions.........................63

How to Develop Responding Skills 64

Engaging Others..64

Empathy..65

Building Relationships and Earning Trust.......................68

Influence 70

PRACTICING EMOTIONAL INTELLIGENCE.............75

What does Emotional Intelligence look like in real life?75

Considering Emotions: Your Own and Others.................75

Manage Your Feelings...76

Respond Instead of React 76

You can Take and Give Feedback 77

Be Authentic, Empathetic, and Helpful.........................78

Keep Your Word 79

Protect Yourself from Other People's Emotions 79

How can Emotional Intelligence Improve My
Relationships? 80

Your Relationship with Yourself................................... 80

Friendships 82

Family Relationships 84

Intimate Relationships... 86

Professional Relationships.. 90

Reduce Fear of Rejection by Keeping Your Sense of Self
Out of it.. 95

Respond Without Reacting to the Emotions Coming at
You.. 96

**TROUBLESHOOTING EMOTIONAL
INTELLIGENCE...100**

Who are You Without Your Problems?..................... 100

Internal Conflict: When Emotions Continue to
Overwhelm You 101

Losing Control of Your Emotions/Behaviour 102

Too Much Empathy 104

Not Hanging on to Positive Emotions 106

Expecting Others to be Emotionally Intelligent......... 107

Dealing with Criticism... 109

Be the Force Field 109

**IN CONCLUSION: ENHANCE YOUR LIFE WITH
EMOTIONAL INTELLIGENCE............................112**

Enhancing Your Life with Emotional Intelligence....... 112

Connecting with People and Deepening Relationships.... 113

Making Better Decisions 114

Living a More Positive Life...................................... 115

Next Steps... 116

ABOUT THE AUTHOR....................................119

INTRODUCTION TO EMOTIONAL INTELLIGENCE

But I'm Just not Good with Feelings

Emotional intelligence. Sounds like an oxymoron that contradicts itself, doesn't it? But that's simply not so. Emotional intelligence means that you use your mind to understand your own emotions and the emotions of others. You use your intelligence to relate to yourself and other people in a way that makes sense and has a positive outcome for both you and those who you interact with.

Everyone can probably name someone they know who is *not* emotionally intelligent. The boss who has no clue the employees are discontented until they go on strike. The spouse that is completely shocked that the other person is asking for a divorce. The kid on the playground who is demanding, always has to

1

win, and is rude or mean to other kids—and then doesn't understand why no one wants to play with them.

These are all examples of people who are emotionally out of it. They don't know what's going on with their own feelings and they certainly don't have a clue what's happening in the minds and hearts of other people. They find it difficult to be empathetic, simply because they have never developed this capacity within themselves.

Yes. Emotional intelligence can be learned. It is not a fixed quality within each person. Just like none of us would have the ability to do higher level math and abstract thinking unless we have trained our minds to know how to do that sort of mental exercise, so too do the people who have emotional intelligence have to work at it to become proficient.

Of course, some people have a natural aptitude at math and so can more easily learn algebra or calculus. But no one would tell someone that they just aren't good at math, so they can never get better at it. That's ridiculous. Anyone can, if they receive instruction and they practice, develop the ability to solve algebra problems.

Just as anyone can develop emotional intelligence, unless they actually have a neurological disorder that prevents them—which some do. But most regular people have the capacity to be more emotionally intelligent than they are right now. Still, if you listen, you'll hear some people swearing up and down that they simply aren't good at feelings or they don't have soft skills. And these people will tell you that that's just how they're built.

Nothing could be further from the truth. Every single person has the ability to be more emotionally intelligent than they are at this moment. Some people have a lot of work to do to acquire the basics of Emotional Intelligence (hereafter referred to as EI) and others are already very skilled. But we can all benefit from continuous improvement in this area in order to be happier and to have better relationships.

Why We all Need to Improve our Emotional Intelligence

Most people have been in a situation in the past where things went badly because they didn't realize how the other person was feeling. And everyone has probably thought, *if only I had known that the other person was upset, I wouldn't have said/done that*.

What you maybe didn't realize was that there were many clues that you didn't notice that could have told you that the person was upset and you could have made different choices that would have led to a better outcome. Emotional intelligence can help us to be aware of what we and others are feeling.

So who cares, you might be asking. It doesn't matter what I'm feeling, it matters what I do. But that's a real fallacy that trips up many people and ensures that they have limited success in their careers, their relationships, and their lives in general.

People who are emotionally intelligent tend to do better with others and that translates into career success and happy relationships. They are also more content because they use the information they have about their own and others' emotions in order to guide their choices. They use their awareness of emotions to choose appropriate behaviour for each situation and they manage their own feelings in order to adapt to different circumstances and to accomplish what they set out to do.

RESEARCH ON EMOTIONAL INTELLIGENCE

It is worth stating for those of you who are skeptical, that there is plenty of current, valid research that proves that a higher EI will make you happier and more successful in your personal and professional relationships.

According to a Psychology Today article[1], emotional intelligence can be learned and retained and EI affects the quality of your relationships with others.

In a Yale University paper in the journal, Social and Personality Psychology Compass, by Marc A. Brackett*, Susan E. Rivers, and Peter Salovey[2], they point out that EI is a protective factor against serious psychological problems in teens.

---

[1] (Brackett, Rivers, & Salovey, 2011)
[2] (Mayer, Salovey, & Caruso, 2002)

Also, in a test called the MSCEIT[3] (Mayer-Salovey-Caruso model of Emotional Intelligence), if dating or married couples scored higher on this test they reported more satisfaction and happiness, whereas the opposite was also true. If the individuals scored lower, they had higher incidences of conflict.

When the term EI first emerged, it was suggested that being more emotionally intelligent would make a person more successful at work and this has also been proven to be true using the MSCEIT.

But Does the Science Matter?

There has been a fair amount of controversy about whether emotional intelligence actually exists, whether it can be measured and if so, how that ought to be accomplished. Though EI has now been proven to be a useful construct that can predict and measure success in life, this book does not attempt to put to rest any of those issues because it doesn't *matter* if it can be proven scientifically or not. Ask yourself honestly the following questions.

1. Have I ever messed up at work or in my personal life and had a fight or other problem as a result of me not paying attention to either how I was feeling or how the other person was feeling?

---

[3] (Mayer, Salovey, & Caruso, 2002)

2. Have I ever overreacted and raised my voice at someone who didn't do anything, just because I was mad about something else but didn't want to acknowledge it?
3. Have I ever suddenly been surprised when someone acts a certain way—gets angry, starts crying, ignores me, etc.—because I had no idea that they had been having these feelings for a long time but I didn't notice?

If you answered no to all three, congratulations, you probably don't need to read this. But if you picked up this book, I'm guessing that you probably answered yes to at least one of those questions. And that means that you need to improve your emotional intelligence. And you can.

It doesn't matter what the scientists are currently arguing about in regards to EI. What matters is that this is a skill that you want to learn.

And that is exactly what this book is proposing to do. Help you learn to better perceive your own and others emotions in order to improve your work and personal life and be happier.

What could be more important than that?

This book will give you the reasons why you want to become more proficient at EI and the tools that will make it possible. You will learn more about understanding and perceiving your own emotions.

We will look at how you can develop your EI to the point where you can feel competent. Then you'll see how to apply emotional intelligence in all your relationships. We'll examine the challenges that come along with being more emotionally intelligent and how you can enhance and improve your life using your new skills.

THE THREE MODELS OF EMOTIONAL INTELLIGENCE

As mentioned before, this book is not going to get into the scientific debates about emotional intelligence. Instead, it will show you how to be more aware of your own and other people's feelings in order to improve your life. But it is useful to have a quick peek at the different models of emotional intelligence that have been put forward, in order for us to better understand how EI works.

Ability Model

In the Ability Model of EI[4], which was developed by Peter Salovey and John Mayer in 2004, emotions are viewed as useful information that can help us

---

[4] (Mayer, Salovey, & Caruso, 2008)

understand and make choices in social situations. This model breaks EI down into four different abilities: perceiving, using, understanding, and managing emotions. These are all interconnected and someone with a high level of EI can use all of these skills at the appropriate moment. These will be discussed in more detail later in the book.

Perceiving emotions is using cues to notice and make sense of feelings in others and one's self. It is the most basic of all EI abilities and it makes possible all of the others. Obviously, you can't use your EI, if you can't detect emotion in the first place.

Using emotions is all about making the most of your own moods to assure that you choose a suitable task for each feeling. Maybe you use a day when you're feeling good to accomplish many tasks on your to-do list. Whereas, if you're experiencing a more sad time, maybe you'll avoid trying to get anything done and instead curl up with a cup of hot chocolate and a good book.

Being able to know what you are feeling can really save you from serious grief because the person who chooses to read when they could have a productive day or the person who tries to get things done when they're feeling down and then experiences guilt instead are both making a big mistake. This could be avoided if only this person had a better connection to their emotions.

Understanding emotions really gets down to the nitty-gritty and is all about being able to differentiate between minute variations in feelings. For example, labeling your feeling as anger can be helpful if you've never even noticed you were upset before. But once you develop more finesse with your emotions, it can help to know if it's frustration or simply irritation that you're feeling. If it's irritation, something is annoying you in the moment. But frustration implies that that annoyance has happened over and over again. If you are able to recognize that it's frustration and then *change* something in your life because of it that is when you know that you are truly becoming an EI master.

Managing emotions is all about not letting our feelings control our responses and behaviors. It is about knowing what's going on inside you and others and being able to decide what actions will serve us best.

Mixed Model

The mixed model, developed by Daniel Goleman[5] in 1998, is based on the following skills: self-awareness, self-management, social awareness, and social interaction. This model posits that emotional intelligence is not something you're born with but that you can become competent at it, like you can

---

[5] (Goleman)

with any other learned skill.

Self-awareness involves recognizing and identifying your own emotions. Self-management means that you can interrupt your own feelings in order to be able to control yourself. It is also about expressing and regulating emotions in an appropriate way.
Social awareness is about reading emotional cues and trying to figure out what they might mean about another person's feelings. Social interaction requires engaging and exploring with others in order to understand them. Then, if required, you can attempt to influence them.

Trait Model

The trait model was developed by Konstantin Vasily Petrides[6] in 2001 and is different from the others in that it asserts that emotional intelligence is simply a part of the personality. This model is not particularly useful to us, because it assumes that emotional intelligence is a fixed bundle of personality traits and so, we will not look at it in detail because the premise of this book is that emotional intelligence is *not* fixed and can be developed. It is only being mentioned here in order for our listing of the EI models to be complete.

---

[6] (Petrides, Pérez-Gonzalez, & Furnham, 2007)

THE NECESSITY OF EI AND HOW YOU CAN IMPROVE YOURS

So now you know. Emotional intelligence is a measurable skill set that allows people who have a high level of EI to succeed in their personal and professional lives. The more EI you have, the better you will do with your colleagues, your spouse, your children, and your friends. Emotional intelligence will give you the ability to understand what's going on inside you and the skill to perceive and hypothesize about what's going on with others. This awareness is kind of like a super power and gives you the knowledge you need to navigate the social waters and emerge from those stormy seas with a favorable outcome.

Everyone can use this to improve their lives and relationships. And don't worry if you think you don't have any emotional intelligence. Sometimes all it takes to become good at something is actually being willing to learn what you need to know and beginning to pay attention to yourself and others. This willingness to try is often the only thing needed to seriously improve your emotional intelligence.

WHAT ARE EMOTIONS?

Everyone talks a lot about emotions but rarely does anyone give much of an explanation of what they are. In this section, we will look at a few definitions of what exactly feelings are.

The Feeling Three

- Emotions are an evolutionary protective mechanism.
- Emotions are just passing through.
- Emotions are great tools but bad bosses.

The Feeling Three: Protection

Emotions are a protective mechanism. They have received a bad reputation over the years but they are *not* the bad guys. Emotions help protect you.

You get scared when something bad happens and those sorts of traumas are then programmed into the nervous system in order to protect you the next time you encounter that situation—for instance you touch fire and get burned, you jump from too high and hurt your leg, you approach a wolf and get bitten—and the fear helps you avoid that danger in the future. Also, anger and the accompanying adrenaline could help you defend yourself in a fight against a wild animal or a hostile human.

Conversely, the opposite is also true. Positive emotions helped people survive by working together. When other humans or animals treated us well, we developed liking or love for them and loyalty. We were then able to co-operate with the other humans or work with animals in order to survive better than any human could on their own.

The problem with this nowadays is that those same emotions that were triggered in life and death situations are now often set off by something as simple as being stuck in traffic or having someone give you feedback on your work. And whereas in the past, those emotions helped us survive, in the present they tend to lead to stress and unhappiness instead.

The Feeling Three: Just Passing Through

Emotions are just passing through. And no, they will not last forever, no matter how bad or good they feel in the moment.

You may have heard the expression: This too shall pass. And though often it is referring to a situation in your life, it could as easily be talking about your emotions. They are passing things and come and go so quickly, that some days you may hardly recognize yourself from minute to minute.

In the morning, you feel cheerful and happy. Then something happens at work or with your family that makes you angry. When the anger passes, you feel sad and apathetic about your life. An hour later, you are confused about how you should live your life in order to avoid all this sadness and anger.

The root of the word emotion is from the word emovere, which means e—out and movere—move. In the 16th century, the word emotion meant a public disturbance. This seems funny but how many public disturbances, even in modern times, are caused by an excess of uncontrolled emotion?

What you need to remember about emotions is that they are passing things. Even a dark mood that comes upon you and seems to set in and want to stay for days, usually doesn't last as long as you think it will when you're in it. Please note that we're not talking about clinical depression here, which can last much longer, but simple sadness or unhappiness. Every emotion is only moving through you and will eventually go. That means that we have to be careful about making decisions when under the influence of certain feelings.

You can probably remember a time when you decided to speak to someone when you were angry and regretted it later. Or quit something when you were feeling down and wished you hadn't made the choice when you were being controlled by your disappointment. Or you even might regret a decision made when you were in a good mood, such as purchasing an item when you were super excited about a new raise. Then when you came back down, you realized that the extra money from the raise maybe ought to have been used to pay down the credit card debt.

Another thing to remember is that your feelings speak a relative truth. Sometimes when your mind says one thing and your heart says another, you don't know which one to believe. In this case, your mind will be deceiving you and the emotion will be telling the truth.

Feelings may protect you in certain circumstances but you also need to protect yourself from your emotions at times by giving your choices some thought over time, rather than making instant decisions based on how you're feeling in the moment.

The Feeling Three: Emotions are Great Tools but Bad Bosses

Emotions are great tools but bad bosses. Use them,

but don't let them use you. Feelings are a tool that we can use to help us navigate life. It is important, though, that the tool does not become the boss. You don't want your feelings in charge and running your life. That's not to say that emotions need to be ignored or suppressed. This is not healthy and will lead to serious problems down the road. Life decisions that are only based on thought and rationale reasoning may be just as wrong for you as choices made by how you happen to be feeling right at this second.

What you need is to use your emotions as a tool to understand what you—and others—really want and need. This will help you make more balanced decisions that will be both smart in a rationale sense and also will lead you to greater happiness, as well. And this is exactly what we will be learning to do in this book.

The Thinking Three: Thoughts, Habits, Perceptions

The way you use your brain has a great effect on your emotions and it's important to remember that how we choose to think has a great impact on how we feel.

How Thoughts Affect Emotions

Let's look at three possible reactions to an event that happens in your life. Your thoughts can be positive or negative and depending on what reaction you have, you will experience different feelings.

The event: You lost your keys.

Reaction #1

Negative - you freak out, rant and rave, run desperately over the house searching, kick yourself for being such an irresponsible person, etc.

These types of thoughts will likely trigger feelings of fear... *What if I don't find them?...* anger and guilt... *I should have taken better care of my things...* and even sadness and disappointment... *I am such a terrible person.*

You could also have a more positive response to the same situation.

Reaction #2

Positive - you realize you've lost your keys, you remain calm, you retrace your steps mentally, you think about where you might have left them and search in those places, you tell yourself that even if they're lost they can be replaced, etc.

These types of thoughts will set off the following sorts of, you guessed it, more positive feelings.

I've lost my keys... not good but not the end of the world either... *I do this too often. From now on, I'm going to keep them always in exactly the same place...* you have a feeling of resolve, that you're going to do better next time... *Now where was I since I saw them last?...* you have a feeling of control—all you have to do is retrace your steps and you will find them.

In the first example, your thoughts gave you deeply negative feelings. Because of this event, you felt afraid, angry, guilty, and ashamed of yourself. In the second example, you felt calm, resolute, and in control. This seemingly negative event has been turned around to become something positive that helps you in your life. You start putting your keys in the same place every time so you can always find them, making you more punctual and giving you the feeling that you can handle and manage your life.

This is just one small example of how controlling your thoughts has a big impact on your feelings. Another thing that affects our emotions is our habits.

How Habits Affect Emotions

Habits are things that you do day in and day out that you don't even think about. Examples of habits that affect your emotional state: having a doughnut with your coffee for breakfast every morning, spending your evenings watching TV, pounding on the steering wheel every time you get stuck in traffic.

How do these habits affect your emotions? If you have a doughnut for breakfast and nothing else, you will inevitably have a post sugar high drop that will make you feel spaced out and irritable. Eating something with more lasting energy instead, would have you feeling steadier and keep your emotions on a more even keel.

If you spend your evenings watching TV, you will be subject to the feelings that those producing the shows and ads want you to feel. An example of the emotions that these people want you to feel might be fear, if you're watching a thriller, or desire food, if you're watching one of those late night junk food commercials. You also will have less energy, the more time you spend sitting and doing nothing. The same evening spent going for a walk or playing a game with your kids would bring you an entirely different set of positive emotions instead.

If every time you get stuck in traffic you have the same angry reaction, this will become a habit and even if you're not in a rush or have nowhere to be, you will still get angry on cue every time you encounter traffic. This is just one example of where we have trained ourselves to have a certain reaction. People have hundreds of habits that bring up negative feelings all day long and one of the things that emotional intelligence will give you is awareness of these habits that make you miserable. Once you have awareness of them, you can then choose to change them in order to improve your life.

Emotions Influence your World View

Think of when you're in a bad mood. Everything seems to be against you. The coffee spilled itself. The table stubbed your toe. And the weather just *had* to rain, didn't it? All because you were having a bad day.

In contrast, when you are feeling happy many times you will not spill the coffee—or if you do, you'll just wipe it up while humming. You likely won't stub your toe. And the rain will seem like a benediction from the sky, watering the flowers and nurturing the earth.

Same circumstances. Very different feelings about them.

When you're feeling bad, you will be more likely to misperceive others and their intentions. When you feel good, you will be more likely to see everything that happens with a positive spin. That is why it is important to manage negative feelings (without suppressing them) and to choose thoughts and habits that will give you positive emotions. It could be the difference between having a mediocre life and having true success and happiness.

What you will learn in this book is how to manage

your emotions to help you perceive the world in a more positive way, in order to improve your life.

Emotion as a Tool is what Emotional Intelligence is all About

As we move into the skills of emotional intelligence, it's important to keep these points about feelings and thoughts in mind.

Feelings are an evolutionary protective mechanism. They are not the bad guys that need to be ignored or suppressed because you don't know what to do with them.

Emotions are also passing, so if you feel bad now, you know from experience that that state is going to change soon and you will feel better. It's important to keep sight of this when you are in the midst of a negative feeling.

Feelings are great tools but bad bosses. You don't want your feelings in charge and making all your decisions for you. But neither do you want to live a life without using your emotions to help you make the best decisions you can.

The Feeling Three reminds us of the nature of emotions—they are not the bad guys, they are fleeting, and they can be used as a tool to improve our lives, if we know how.

On the other hand, thoughts and habits contribute greatly to how you feel and how you see the events of your life. It's important to carefully choose what you think and do because it has a huge influence on your happiness and success.

The Thinking Three remind you to be mindful of your thoughts because the way you think affects how you feel and your very perception of the world. Thoughts affect your life deeply, so make sure you're thinking good ones.

Now, let's move on to the next section where we will begin looking at the Four Rs of Emotional Intelligence: recognition, regulation, reading signals, and responding. With the Four Rs in hand, you will be well-equipped to deal with your own emotions and be able to build better relationships with others.

LEARNING EMOTIONAL INTELLIGENCE

The Four R's of Emotional Intelligence

One way of learning the skills needed for emotional intelligence is to remember the four Rs—Recognition, Regulation, Reading signals, and Responding.

Recognition means recognizing what emotions you are experiencing.

Regulation is being able to control your actions when experiencing those emotions.

Reading signals refers to picking up on the cues that others are giving you about how they are feeling.

Responding is how you interact with other people in

order to both build a good relationship with them and also influence them.

In the next section, we will look at each R in more detail and you will learn tools and techniques for become more adept at each EI skill.

The First R: Recognition

Recognition means recognizing what emotions you are experiencing.

What is Recognition in Emotional Intelligence?

Recognition is simply being aware of your emotions. That seems easy. Often, though, it is anything but. If you are minutely aware of every feeling you have as you have it, then congratulations, you already have the skill of Recognition. But if you're anything like most people, at least some of the time you are running on autopilot and you don't realize you're angry until you're yelling at the kids who didn't do anything or you collapse in tears over some small thing your spouse said or you've sat for an hour staring at the wall because you're confused about what your next move should be.

Many people have a peripheral awareness of how they're feeling, in that they notice when they're experiencing really negative emotions that make them feel extremely bad. Though truth be told, most of us simply don't pay any attention to the smaller and more intricate emotions. We ignore the irritation at waiting in line or even shrug off something positive like the satisfaction we feel at having crossed something off our To-Do list, in our rush to get to the next thing.

Recognition is about paying attention not only to the external world but also your *internal* world.

Why do You Need Recognition?

Why do you need the skill of being able to identify your emotions? Well, the fact is that if you can't recognize how you are feeling then the rest of the emotional intelligence skills will be impossible to develop.

Recognition of what you are feeling is a basic ability that is necessary to build all the other skills. Like in swimming, if you can't float, there's no way you're going to be able to learn front crawl. The first thing you have to be able to do is float on the water and the rest follows.

It is the same thing with emotional intelligence. If you can't even recognize your own emotions when they're happening, you're not going to be evaluating the appropriateness of those feelings—because you don't even know you're having them! How can you use emotions appropriately if you aren't aware of them? And forget being able to understand others and influence them. If you don't know what's going

28

on inside you, how in the world will you ever have a clue what's going on inside someone else?

What if you were a carpenter and your hammer was invisible to you? How could you use that tool if you couldn't even see it? That's why you need to be able to recognize your own emotions. You can't use them as a tool for improving your life if you can't perceive them at all.

How do I Develop Recognition?

Recognizing your emotions is all about paying attention to your life. And the trick to that is to be more present. When your head is already on your next task, you don't even know how you're feeling about what you're doing *right now*. So bring your attention back to the moment at hand. Really look or listen or feel what you are doing externally—the report, the dishes, or the drive to work.

Then take that a step further and sense what's happening internally. What feeling is present? If you sense anger, can you drill down and get really specific? Is it irritation, frustration, rage, or a minor annoyance? What about that fear in your belly? Is it anxiety, dread, maybe even something as strong as terror? Most of us are afraid that if we feel our emotions, they will worsen but that is not usually the case. Often, feelings simply want to be acknowledged and then they will go away.

As a simple exercise, take a moment right now and sense how you're feeling. Go ahead. Close your eyes. If you identify the emotion as one of the big three— happy, sad, angry—could you be more specific? If you're angry, can you pinpoint the more distinct emotion within the anger?

In order to get in the habit of checking in on your emotional state, you can tie it to something you do all the time. Such as, every time you walk through a doorway, see how you're feeling. Or if you climb stairs frequently, every time you go up or down do a quick check in and see what you're feeling. What about setting a reminder on your phone every couple of hours? You could make it into a bit of a game to try and remain aware of your internal state as often as possible. We will touch on a lot more tools and exercises later on in the book.

The Second R: Regulation

Regulation is being able to control your actions when experiencing emotions.

What is Regulation?

Most adult humans have learned at least a small amount of regulation in regards to their emotions. If you can function, even minimally, in society, then you must have learned to regulate yourself somewhat.
Remember when you used to stomp your feet and

scream in the grocery store because you wanted candy? You never did that? Well, many toddlers or young children do. But then they learn to control that response to being denied something. You may want something quite badly as an adult but you likely will not be stomping your feet or screaming. That is regulation.

That said. Many of us could use an upgrade when it comes to the level of emotional regulation we are capable of. Only using basic emotional regulation is not good enough for anyone who has chosen to read this book. You want to do better. You want to be more.

In an emotionally intelligent person, regulation is being able to use and express emotions appropriately, which many of the people reading this book are already capable of, though this can be refined and deepened. More advanced practitioners of emotional intelligence are able to stop emotional reactions *without suppressing them* and they can also bring up certain emotional states that will be useful to them in certain situations that they may find themselves in.

For example, being able to stop—not suppress—an angry emotional reaction so that you don't yell at your child who has just broken their smartphone. Or being able to bring up a truly peaceful feeling in this moment—even though you're going through something difficult in your life situation—so that you

31

can be present and happy for your brother on his birthday.

Many of us have the basic skills of Regulation but we need some training in order to develop some real finesse in regulating.

Why You Need Regulation.

Because many of us have the basics of emotional regulation that we learned as children or teenagers, we think that we're good. We don't need to develop any more. But that's like someone learning only the basic phrases in a language and stopping there. Sure, the person can get by, but they will never have the depth of communication that they would have if they had made an effort to truly become fluent. They will never connect with others who speak that language in the way that they might have. And it's the same with emotional regulation.

Though most functioning adults possess the self-control to stop themselves from hitting a child. How many think nothing of giving them heck verbally? It's called a tongue-lashing for a reason. Because, for a child, there is little difference in the pain they feel. Sure, it's a different kind of pain—emotional instead of physical—but it's still suffering. Imagine if you could control your emotions enough that you could stop yourself from talking to the child about their actions until you were calm and thinking rationally again?

And it's not only parents with children that have this issue with speaking hastily and regretting it later. Many people's biggest regrets center around taking back something they said while under the influence of a strong emotion. What if you had enough control to choose *before* you said those words that would destroy a relationship forever?

Calling up certain emotions is also useful in getting ahead in life. There is plenty of research that says that pessimists and those who have a negative outlook just don't accomplish as much as those who are happy and positive. We are not talking here about suppressing negative emotions and then playing Pollyanna and only *pretending* to have a positive feeling.

Evoking emotions is not pretending. It is having the tools to release negative feelings and then replacing those feelings with genuine positive emotions. There is no making things up. People who can do this are honestly changing their internal state. And being able to do this has many benefits to your life.

How Do I Develop Regulation?

Developing Regulation in adults is usually more of a deepening of the self-control skills you already have. And also learning to both release negative emotions and evoke positive ones.

Using and expressing emotions properly is something that we know how to do but these are skills that we could really stand to master. Sure, we have the basic phrases of the language, but it's time to move past that and really start talking. This is mostly about getting better at self-control. Self-control is like a muscle. The more you use it, the stronger it will get.

And in most cases, the control the average person is looking for is in their words, such as being able to stop themselves from being grumpy to the waiter when they bring the wrong order or holding back when they really want to dump all of their sadness on a friend. This is not to say that you shouldn't communicate how you are feeling but choosing the appropriate time and the *way* you express yourself is important.

We also want more self-control often when it comes to things we're *not* doing but we want to. We feel lazy, lethargic, and depressed so we don't go to the gym, even though we know that would make us feel better. Regulation can help with that if we use it to evoke a more positive feeling, which in turn may get us moving.

Try this regulation technique the next time you get angry with someone. It could be a spouse, co-worker, child, or driver who cut you off. When you have recognized that you are angry, do the following. Take a deep breath then breathe out as you count slowly down from ten to zero. Then take another deep breath. At this point, you may speak or take some action in the situation. This short exercise should only take maybe five to ten seconds, but will give you enough control to respond to the situation instead of reacting.

Later in the book, we will be diving deep into exactly how to develop more self-control, methods for stopping negative emotional cycles, and learning to evoke positive emotions.

The Third R: Reading Signals

Reading signals refers to picking up on the cues that others are giving you about how they are feeling.

What Does it Mean to Read Signals?

Reading signals is all about body language. People give signals constantly that show you how they are feeling, if you only know how to read the messages they are sending. The main ways you can discern what others are feeling require paying attention to the following: eye contact, the expression of the face, tone of voice—this includes both volume and pitch—personal space, touch, gestures, posture and appearance, as well as many other subtle non-verbal cues.

The way people make eye contact can tell you a lot about how they are feeling. Did you ever meet someone who wouldn't meet your eye? How did you feel about that person? Would you trust them? What about someone who can't *hold* eye contact? This often conveys shiftiness in our minds, whether the person is questionable or not. And then there's the person who makes appropriate eye contact. This is the person that you connect with and want to talk to more because you feel that they see you.

Sometimes body language does not show what the person is really feeling. But those instances are few and far between. There's a reason lie detector tests have been developed. That's because people have certain body language and physiological responses when they are not being honest. This is measurable. And you can pick up on it, too.

Of course, we're not only talking about being able to tell if someone is lying. But if a person's dishonesty is obvious when you know what to look for, it is not a big leap to realize that other emotions can be seen in a person's body language as well.

Reading signals is all about getting better at picking up on cues that the other person is giving you that show how they are feeling.

Why do You Need to be Able to Read Signals?

Many of us have kicked ourselves at being fooled by another person. But you might have also wished that you had known that a person was sad, so that you wouldn't have said that inappropriate comment that upset them more. Or sometimes you might wish you'd known that the person needed us to push more or maybe back off as the case may be. But we didn't do the right thing because we didn't know what the other person was feeling or what they needed in that moment.

In some cases, it might have caused an argument or a rift in the relationship. Other times it may cost you the promotion at work. Sometimes it might have cost you actual money because someone swindled you. In every instance, though, you could have made better decisions if you had had insight into what was going on with the person in front of you.

And that is why you need to have the skill of Reading Signals. If you can correctly interpret how people are feeling a large percentage of the time, then you will be more successful in your interactions with others. Obviously, you won't be right all the time but that is what the Responding section is about. Once we think we know how the other person is feeling, we need to confirm whether we are right or wrong in our assessment.

How Do I Develop the Ability to Read Signals?

Once again, Reading Signals is about paying attention. Just like in Recognition we have to be aware of our own internal state, in Reading Signals we have to perceive another's internal state by the signals they are sending us.

In order to begin to pick up on another person's emotional state, it is important for us to be present with what is actually happening. If we are thinking about what we're going to make for supper while our child is telling us about their day, we will most likely miss the tremble in their voice when they mention that they had a fight with their best friend. We may miss the way their eyes drop to the floor. And we may not hear the sigh after they say the words. We continue going about our day but then wonder why our child is freaking out about the fact that they got the wrong colored cup.

If we had been paying attention, then we might have spoken with our child about the incident and helped them to recognize their own emotions and make a decision about what to do. Maybe they want to call their friend and apologize or make a card that says they're sorry to give their friend at school tomorrow. In this scenario, the freak out never happens because we have helped our child successfully navigate their feelings.

A professional example might be that you say good morning to a co-worker that you're close to at work but you are already thinking about the meeting you have later in the day. Because you're not present, you don't notice that your co-worker's jaw is set, they are breathing a little more quickly than normal, and their eyebrows are drawn together. You also ignore the fact that their voice is tense and their response to your good morning is terse. Later, when you ask for the report you need for your meeting, you are surprised when your co-worker snaps at you that they don't have it ready and to leave them alone. If they don't actually get you what you need for your meeting, this may negatively affect you at work.

But let's look at how the situation might have played out if you had been using emotional intelligence skills. You notice your co-worker seems off when you say good morning and you ask if there's anything wrong and if they'd like to talk about it. The person lets loose about how upset they are about a fender-bender they had this morning. You listen and offer a possible solution or maybe you just commiserate with them. The person feels better and thanks you for helping them talk about their troubles. They remember that they still owe you that report and promise to get right on it, so that you'll have it for the meeting. They may remember your small kindness and continue to help you and support you into the future as well, because that's what people do.

This small act of truly paying attention to others is how you learn to Read Signals. It can pay big dividends at work and at home and it also makes you a nicer person in general because it lessens the natural self-centeredness that we all are guilty of at one time or another.

This is how developing emotional intelligence can

positively affect your professional as well as your personal life and it's why you need to learn to read the cues, which other people are constantly sending.

The Fourth R: Responding

Responding is how you interact with other people in order to both build a good relationship with them and also influence them.
What is Responding?

Responding is all about using Recognition, Regulation, and Reading Signals in order to build positive relationships and influence others.

Responding is when you take all the information you've collected about how you are feeling and how the other person is feeling and the general information about the social situation in which you find yourself. Then you engage the other person, usually in conversation and build a relationship, sometimes in order to influence them to do something you want them to.

This is where we put it all together and you use the knowledge and skills you have about understanding emotions and then put them to good use.

For instance, you use your emotional intelligence skills to navigate a tricky negotiation at work, using your new abilities to pick up on what the other parties are feeling to help you achieve a positive outcome.

Or you pay closer attention to your spouse at the end of your work day and—by using your newly learned emotional intelligence—what would have usually ended up in a fight, instead turns into a conversation about how they're feeling about the finances, and ends up with a nice dinner and a movie. No fight needed.

Responding is all about taking the knowledge and information that you perceive in yourself and the cues you pick up from others and using them to strengthen and improve your relationships.

Why do You Need Responding?

Responding is a big part of how we fulfill the basic human need of connecting with other people. It is perhaps an indication of how social skills, that were natural a long time ago, now have to be relearned by modern homo sapiens.

Responding is straightforward human interaction between two people. It's about paying attention to the other person. It's about exchanging ideas and connecting. This is the most basic of human skills that we learn when we are babies. Some of us have got so caught up in our complicated lives that we have forgotten this most instinctive of skills—human connection.

So, why do you need responding? Because you're human and everyone needs to connect with others. Getting good at this can have positive consequences in your personal and work life. Because you have connected with people, they will be more likely to listen to you and do what you'd like them to. Of course, we have to be careful that this doesn't become the main thing when it should only be a side benefit.

You do not want to build relationships *only* to get people to do what you want. People often want to help or follow others that they like, admire, or love. Being able to influence people is the by-product of a healthy relationship. It shouldn't be the end game. If you are only building relationships because you want people to do something, others will sense it and feel that you are not genuine. Build relationships because you want to connect with people. Then when you need a favor from them or you need them to listen to you, your loved one or co-worker will be more likely to do so.

How Do I Develop Responding Skills?

This can be easy or difficult depending on whether you are an introvert or extrovert. Extroverts are naturally better at developing their Responding skills because they gain energy from interacting with other people. Introverts, on the other hand, find it energy draining to be with others and they gain energy from being alone. So, this makes it more of a challenge to develop Responding skills as an introvert but it by no means makes it impossible. Introverts simply have to be mindful of their energy levels and not do too much interacting all at once.

Developing Responding skills is about engaging others in conversation, reading the signals they're sending and using your empathy to understand them. Then you build relationships by connecting with the other person. Once you have developed a relationship, then you can think about influencing them. Without a relationship, though, it is going to be difficult to get other people to do what you want them to.

Many people, though, have jobs that require them to get other people to do what they want them to and not what they want. If you are a manager, a teacher, a doctor, or anyone who has to get others to do what you say, then you will understand how challenging this can sometimes be. But there is no doubt that if you have a positive relationship with the other person, then that you will have better chance of having them listen to you and do what you ask.

Ways you can start practicing your Responding skills right away is to pay closer attention to the next person you interact with. See if you can read their signals. Then when you engage with them, try verifying that what you've observed is indeed how they're feeling.

For example, you may notice that someone is smiling and humming, their shoulders back, their eyes bright and you may rightly assume that they are happy. When you have a conversation with them, it may come out right away with the person telling you what they are so happy about. Or you may comment that they seem chipper and that may start a conversation about what happened to make them so.

Of course, this is a very crude and obvious example, but for people whose responding skills need work, it can be a good place to start.

DEVELOPING EMOTIONAL INTELLIGENCE

In this chapter you will learn techniques for developing the 4Rs to improve your emotional intelligence skills.

How to Develop Recognition Skills

Recognition skills are all about paying attention to how you are feeling. In this section, you will also learn to spot certain circumstances or situations that always trigger a certain emotion—either negative or positive. And lastly, we will look at using your critical faculties to evaluate whether a reaction is appropriate or not.

Noticing Feelings

The first step is noticing. You cannot develop any other emotional intelligence skill without first being able to notice your emotions. Just as you have to stand before you can walk, you have to notice your feelings before you can do anything with them. But how are you supposed to notice your feelings if you are busy all day thinking about what your mind might call *more important things.*

There are three techniques you can use to develop the ability to notice how you are feeling.

- Decide to do it.
- Tie it to an ingrained habit.
- Use technology to remind you.

Noticing Feelings: Decide to Notice Your Feelings Without Judgement

The first technique is just telling yourself that you are going to start noticing your feelings. This will turn on your reticular activating system in the brain. You know how when you decide to get pregnant or buy a certain model of car, all of a sudden you start seeing women with bellies or Volkswagen Beetles everywhere?

This is your reticular activating system at work. We have billions of pieces of information coming at us every second and our brain has to decide what to pay attention to and what to filter out. When you tell your brain that you have a certain goal, such as noticing your feelings, then it will start paying attention and begin sending you the information it receives that pertains to that goal.

Simply making the decision to notice how you are feeling, will make you more aware of your feelings. Congratulate yourself every time you notice and this will continue to create a positive feedback loop that will help you notice even more. It's important at this point not to judge how you're feeling. If your mind criticizes you every time you notice yourself having a negative feeling, then you will not want to notice your emotions anymore and any hope of improving your emotional intelligence will be wiped away.

So, decide to notice your feelings without judgment and you will soon be paying a lot more attention to your emotions.

Noticing Feelings: Tie the Noticing to an Ingrained Habit

This is an old trick to develop new habits. You link a new habit you want to form to an old habit that's already a part of your life.

So, maybe you tie noticing your feelings to drinking your morning cup of coffee or tea. Or maybe you decided that every time you go through a doorway or up a flight of stairs, you'll notice. Or maybe you think it would be useful to pay attention every time you get in your car. You need to decide what you think will work for you.

At first you may need to place reminders on your stair rail or your steering wheel. Do what you have to and just get started. Soon you'll be doing it automatically. And that awareness will spread to other times and places as well.

Noticing Feelings: Use Technology to Remind You

Maybe the habit method doesn't work for you. That's fine. Many people these days have smartphones. If that's you, then set a repeating reminder to go off every hour or two. Whenever you see that reminder, you tell yourself to stop and pay attention to how you are feeling.

You don't have a smartphone? How about a watch with a timer? An egg timer? An alarm clock? Maybe just ask a friend or family member who understands what you're trying to do to ask you how you're feeling whenever you see them. Or write yourself notes that you will see periodically.

Do what you have to do to get started. Once you have begun the process, you will get in the habit of checking in with yourself frequently and it will become natural.

Identify and Observe the Feeling

Noticing your feelings is tough at first. But once you

get in the habit, you can begin the real work. The first step is to identify your feelings. This sounds easy.

I am mad.
I am sad.
I am glad.

If you are really going to become proficient at emotional intelligence, you have to get into the details of your feelings. Admittedly, you may not want to do this because sometimes those emotions can be unpleasant. But if you want the rewards, you have to do the work. And that means getting very granular about how you are feeling.

If you're feeling mad, is it...
Anger
Annoyance
Irritation
Exasperation
Displeasure
Indignation
Rage

If you're feeling sad, is it...
Unhappiness
Sorrow
Dejection
Regret
Depression
Misery

Low spirits
Melancholy
Gloominess
Heartache
Grief
Despair

If you're glad, is it...
Contentment
Satisfaction
Cheerfulness
Delight
Glee
Happiness
Joy

Once you have begun noticing your emotions, it's important that you try as much as you can to be very specific about how you are feeling in order to achieve the highest levels of emotional intelligence. There are hundreds of emotions but how many are you really aware of throughout your day? Developing your Emotional Intelligence will help you to become more cognizant of your feelings and more in tune with your inner state.

Identify Emotional Triggers

As a bonus, when you start noticing and identifying your feelings, you may also start to pay attention to when and where and with whom you experience those feelings.

You may realize that you always feel happy when you hear a certain song, angry when you're commuting, or sad around a specific person.

These sorts of epiphanies can really help you improve your life. You can listen to that song that makes you feel happy when you need to have a positive mindset and good energy. If you identify songs that change your emotional state, you can then use them when you want to feel differently.

You may start listening to audio books or calming music to help you feel more peaceful and less irritated when you're driving to work. This will not only help you feel better but could also prevent an accident.

Occasionally when you realize that someone in your life is toxic to you, you may need to end the friendship. Or if that person makes you feel sad, you may want to spend less time with them or shorter periods of time, while still maintaining the relationship.

You don't have to go out and end all your friendships because once you went home sad after having dinner with your depressed roommate from college. But consider how circumstances and situations make you feel and decide whether you can perhaps deal with the trigger so that it disappears or eliminate the situation completely.

Evaluate the Appropriateness of Your Reactions

As you start becoming more emotionally intelligent, you may notice that some of your reactions to certain situations are out of proportion to what actually happened. When you notice these out of proportion feelings, it's important not to give in to the urge to act on them. In the following chapter, you will learn techniques to help with self-control in order to learn how to do this. It's not easy but will save you much pain in your life if you can do it.

How to Develop Regulating Skills

Regulation is all about self-control. In this chapter, you will learn how to use and express your emotions appropriately. You will also learn how to stop emotional reactions without suppressing them and also how to change your emotional state.

How to Use or Express Your Emotions

A note of caution

Let's begin this section with a note of caution about using and expressing your emotions. It is sometimes difficult to maintain control when in the thrall of a powerful emotion. If you feel like the emotional reaction is too strong, then you should not try using it or expressing it.

Instead, observe the emotion, without thinking about it or acting on it. Once you are in full control again, that is when you can think about using or expressing that emotion.

It cannot be said too many times...Please, do not attempt to use or express your emotions when they are too strong because you will almost always do or say something that will cause you or others pain and that you will later regret.

Using Your Emotions Constructively

That said, if the emotion is not too strong and it is under your control, you can harness it in order to accomplish things. Some ways that people use their emotions are the following.

1. Taking the sadness you feel and writing a song about it.
2. Capitalizing on those positive feel good vibes and crossing things off on your To-Do list.
3. Using your angry energy to do fifty push-ups, fifty crunches, and thirty burpies.
4. Taking the outrage you feel about an unfair situation and funneling that energy into doing something to help change it.
5. Channeling your worry about your financial problems into taking action to improve your money situation.
6. Feeling guilty about something that you've done wrong can push you to go apologize or make

things right with the other person.

Expressing Your Emotions

Once again, please do not express your emotions if they are too powerful and out of your control. Everyone has done this in the past and rarely do we feel that it turned out well. But if the emotions are not too strong, under your control, or you have calmed down from a really strong feeling, then you can consider expressing yourself to another person.

Many times in your life, expressing how you feel is not actually necessary because once the emotion has subsided and you regain perspective, you realize that it was your reaction that was the problem, not what the other person did.

Now sometimes the other person *has* done something wrong and you *do* need to speak up about it. If that is the case, then please consider using the following steps to communicate how you feel/felt clearly and without making the other person defensive. If the other person starts defending themselves, the conversation is over because then they will not be able to hear what you have to say. It is important to communicate in a way that the other person can actually hear.

First of all, be clear about how you feel and do not avoid the issue. If you do this, the other person will probably not realize what you are trying to say. Or they will misunderstand what you were trying to communicate.

Also, using 'I' statements is another way to keep a conversation from escalating into an argument. An 'I' statement has three parts.
First, state the behaviour that you are commenting on.

"You didn't text to check in when you were out last night."

Second, tell how you feel about that using the word 'I'.

"I felt worried."

Third, explain why you felt the way you did.

"I thought that something might have happened to you."

Don't say this:

Um, so, yeah, you didn't call to check in when you were out last night.

Or this:

You didn't text to check in last night, you're grounded/dumped!

Say this: *When you don't text me to check in, I feel worried because I think something bad might have happened to you.*

This beginning to a conversation does not point fingers. It focuses on how you feel not what the other person did. And it has a much better chance of you getting what you want, which is for the other person to listen to your concerns and hopefully change their behaviour.

You may have to practice in your mind using an 'I' statement in the beginning because it feels a bit awkward at first. But when you see the difference in the response it gets, you will no doubt start using them all the time. 'I' statements can truly improve your relationships and allow you to influence people far more successfully than if you use the traditional 'you' statements that point fingers and assign blame.

It is often not necessary to express our emotions at all. What is actually needed is to properly manage them. But when it is appropriate to tell someone how you feel, use an 'I' statement in order to keep the person from getting defensive and tuning you out.

Releasing Emotional Reactions: Put Them in the Feelings Pot

The problem with strong emotional reactions is that there is usually a feedback loop with the mind. If it was only an emotion, you could feel it, let it go, and move on. But more often than not, the emotion feeds the thoughts, which in turn feed the feeling again and you get stuck. You can't get rid of the unpleasant emotion and you can't stop thinking about what made you feel that way, either.

The way to stop emotional reactions and release the negative feelings is to observe them without thinking. This is trickier than it sounds, since we spend most of our waking time thinking. But the way to do it is to use your own mind to control itself.

The first step is to focus on the emotion. Usually it will be in the body somewhere. Once you have that, then imagine a big pot around the emotion. The pot holds the feeling and you hold the pot. This can give you a little bit of space around the emotion and allow you to break the feedback loop from the mind.

It's important that every time your mind tries to pull you back in to thinking about what happened, that you ignore it and focus on the pot that's holding the emotion. Tell your mind.

I'm holding my pot right now. Come back later.

You will be surprised how easily stuck feelings subside when you pay attention to them. It's as if they are babies and they need your attention. Once they have it, they stop crying.

Just hold your emotion in your pot and give it some

attention, soon you'll notice that it's subsiding. Unless you feed it with your thoughts, then it will likely spring back to life again. It's important to tell your thoughts to come back later and pay attention to your pot of feelings.

This will stop the feelings and will allow them to dissipate on their own. No suppression needed. You don't want to suppress your emotions because what happens is that you squash them into an already full closet and then the next time you open the closet door again, they all come bursting out in a crazy explosion. That's not stopping your feelings, it's just avoiding them.

This exercise will ensure that your emotions go away and don't come back. And is much better than either expressing them inappropriately or suppressing them. Put your feelings in the pot and watch them and you will soon be free of them.

How to Change your Emotional State

When changing your emotional state you need to begin by releasing any negative emotions using your Feelings Pot exercise. Once you are sure that the emotion has completely subsided, then you can move on to changing your state to something more positive.

Take out a piece of paper and sit down and write out everything that you enjoy and that makes you feel good. It could be songs, places, people, or activities. Once you have a good long list, cross off the ones that are not usually available. For instance, going on a trip to the Caribbean may make you feel good, but it's not something you can use every day to change your mood.

Some common examples of things that might help you to move into a more positive emotional state are...

- Listening to upbeat, happy music.
- Playing an instrument or singing.
- A quiet place, like a park or a hiking trail, or maybe a favourite room in your house.
- Exercising—maybe going for a walk, a run, a workout at the gym, or dancing, canoeing, or some other activity that you enjoy.
- Chatting with a particularly positive friend, who always makes you feel better.
- Doing a craft or hobby, such as painting, knitting, woodworking, etc.
- Playing a game—a video game or a board game with a friend, or it could even be solitaire.
- Other activities that make you feel happy.

What all these have in common is that they all have an aspect that involves one of the senses, which is calming. Or it is a relaxing activity that allows you to release the negative emotion more easily and allow a more positive feeling to emerge.

When changing your emotional state, it's important to not have a Pollyanna type attitude and just paste on a smile, while inside you are dying of misery. No. It's about holding your emotions in your Feelings Pot and giving them the attention they need to dissolve. Then when you have released the negative emotion, you use activities that make you happy to replace the negative feeling with a positive one.

How to Develop the Skills to Read Other People's Signals

Reading signals involves being able to notice and interpret social cues. This involves understanding body language, tone of voice, and other non-verbal communication such as the following.

- Eye contact
- Facial expressions
- Personal space
- Touch
- Gestures
- Posture
- Appearance
- Tone of voice: both volume and pitch

If you are new to paying attention to these sorts of things, the aspects of body language that will give you the most information are eye contact, facial expressions, posture, and tone of voice. We will look at all three in this chapter.

Eye Contact

The way some one does or doesn't meet your eyes can tell you a lot about that person and their internal state. If they are able to make eye contact and hold it naturally while you converse with them, that shows that the person is probably confident and has normal self-esteem and social skills. It also shows that they are either good at managing their emotions or they are feeling good.

Someone who can't meet your eye or keeps looking away could be doing that either because they are uncomfortable in the social situation or possibly they have done something they shouldn't have and feel guilty about it and can't meet your eyes. The bad guys in books are always described as shifty-eyed for a reason.

A person who does not meet your eyes at all is giving off big keep-away vibes. In some cases, you may receive this signal from someone and listen to it— keeping your distance. But sometimes, if it's someone you know and care about that's sending these *leave me alone* signals, it could actually be a cry for help and they actually need someone a lot because they are feeling very bad inside.

These are a just a couple of examples of the myriad of situations that eye contact can give you some insight into. It seems complicated but that's just because it is being dissected here. In real life, humans are designed to read non-verbal communication and we do it easily. You don't want to think about it too much and instead simply pay attention to your hunches, as these will often be correct.

Facial Expressions and Posture

Facial expressions and posture are pretty straightforward and we've all been reading them since we were babies. Sagging forward with the body and shoulders, mouth drooping, and eyes downcast are all signs a person is feeling sad. Tension and tightness in the face and body, red face, eyebrows drawn together, and heavier breathing are all showing a person is angry. Bright eyes, a smiling mouth, chest lifted, and straight posture are indications of happiness.

Tone of Voice: Volume and Pitch

Of course, tone of voice is also something we have all had a lot of practice interpreting. When someone has raised their voice, usually they are happy or angry. If their voice is quiet, that can indicate sadness or calm.

Often when people get upset, the pitch of their voice goes up. Maybe that's where the expression *calm down* comes from. And perhaps that's why people always use a low voice when trying to help someone who is upset or anxious.

Reading Signals and Making Decisions

Once you have decided how you *think* a person is feeling, then you need to look at what options are available and choose an appropriate action.

It is best if you attempt to confirm that what you think is happening is really what's happening by asking the person how they are. But sometimes people will not tell the truth about how they are feeling with their words, but their body language doesn't lie.

You come into the house, take off your coat, throw yourself on the couch, and turn on the TV. Your spouse comes in and you ask how they are. They say that they are fine but something tells you that they aren't fine at all. When you start to pay attention, you notice the eyebrows frowning, their arms are crossed on their chest, their lips are tight, and their breathing irregular. When you ask what's wrong, finally, your spouse says that it's Valentine's Day, which you've clearly forgotten. Oops.

Though the other person said they were fine, you knew that they weren't because their words and their body language did not match.

If you can confirm that your hunch about how they are feeling is correct, that is always better than going on assumptions. Because certain body language can be mistaken and we can also misinterpret what we see.

But even if you're not sure that a person is upset, you can always be more careful and considerate, just in case. That sort of behaviour is not often going to go awry.

How to Develop Responding Skills

The skills of responding involve engaging others in social behaviour, empathizing in order to understand them, building relationships, and as a by-product of this prosocial behaviour earning others' trust and being able to influence them.

Engaging Others

Engaging others, just means interacting with other people. Emotional intelligence is about first understanding how you—and the other person as much as possible—are feeling. Then you move into interacting with the other person in order to build a relationship.

It all sounds very boring and black and white on paper, but this is the stuff that life is made of. You may hear people saying that someone is a lone wolf but it's not true. Humans are social creatures. Our continued existence is based on the fact that we were able to gather together in social groups and co-operate to survive.

What do people do when they're not working? They socialize. Even in today's connected world, people who don't connect with real people are watching TV shows or movies about people or they're connecting with people digitally.

Engaging with others is what we do.
That said, our modern world has made perfectly natural activities, like socializing with others, difficult for some. There are people who find it uncomfortable to be around other people and if this is you, you may like to read another book in the *Conversationalist* series about *Small Talk*, which goes into more detail about how to talk to other people (*Small Talk: How to Start a Conversation, Truly Connect with Others and Make a Killer First Impression* by Diane Weston).
.

Empathy

What is empathy? Empathy is when you can understand and feel what another person is experiencing. Every human being has empathy. Yes, every single person, unless the person has something wrong with their brain.

Scientists have discovered something in the brain called mirror neurons. These neurons are responsible for how you immediately feel sad and quiet when you walk into a funeral or pumped up and happy when you enter a party.

Mirror neurons are cells in the brain that are there to make you more social. Vlad Tarko[7] explains mirror neurons as the following: "Mirror neurons are activated both when one does something and when one observes somebody else doing the same thing. Thus, they represent the neurological mechanism that allows us to put ourselves in the shoes of others."

People feel more understood and make better connections with others who they feel understand them. Mirror neurons are one of the ways that evolution has made sure that we continue to understand and empathize with other people.

But what about murderers and others who hurt people? Surely they don't have empathy? Sorry. But everyone *has* empathy. What happens is that it can be covered up and suppressed. The mind has ways of telling itself stories so that it doesn't feel the pain, guilt, and shame of its actions.

Then again, most people do not fall into that category. And this book is for regular people with regular emotional responses and without any super serious mental conditions. That said, you cannot now say that you just aren't empathetic. Every normal person has mirror neurons.

---

[7] (Tarko, 2006)

And once again, the way to activate this part of the brain and use the information it has, is to pay attention. If you find you have difficulty putting yourself in another person's shoes and understanding their situation, there are a couple exercises you can try.

The first is just using your imagination to pretend that you're that person and seeing what life looks like from their eyes. You did it all the time when you were a kid. You pretended to be a grown up, a super hero, someone from the past, or your favourite character from a TV show. It's the same thing. Your mind can be used to understand other people, if you use it that way. Just close your eyes for a second and imagine what it must be like to see the world from their position. Even a few moments of visualizing in this way can give you a completely different perspective on someone.

The second way of developing empathy is by reading a book.

What? Reading a book?

Yes. Reading a book.

Reading fiction stories is one of the best ways to put yourself in someone else's shoes because your mind is literally seeing the world from the character's eyes. Be sure and choose a book that has a character that is different from you—different gender, different race, different socio-economic status. And, yes, it has to be reading. There is a different process that goes on in the mind when you read, as opposed to watch a movie or TV show. When you read, your mind is so immersed in the experience, that it feels as though it is actually experiencing the character's life. In video, there is always a little more distance.

So, if you really want to develop your empathy, start reading books that give you a different perspective. If you're female, read books from a man's perspective and vice versa. This can honestly give you a window into another person's soul and will develop your ability to be empathetic in real life.

Building Relationships and Earning Trust

Engaging others and being a pleasant and likeable person to be around is a good start in building relationship. Being empathetic to another's situation is an excellent way to continue strengthening that relationship. But that is only the beginning.

Spending time with others is the only way to build relationships. There is no short cut. You can't just jump into a brand new relationship and expect it to have the strength and trust of an established one. You also cannot expect the other person to instantly trust you and be influenced by you.

People seem to forget this. Especially perhaps those

in helping professions that deal with children. We seem to think that just because *we* know we're likeable and trustworthy, that kids should instantly like and trust us. That's not how it works.

Building relationships is about showing over and over, time and again, that you care about the other person, that you will be there for them when they need you, and that you can be trusted.

Sometimes people think that they can put in a quick bit of effort and then reap huge rewards in their personal and professional relationships. But that isn't the real world. A parent that isn't there for their kid's day in and day out for their whole life, can't pop in all of a sudden and expect the kid to love them the way they would if that person had been there for them when they were at their best and also when they weren't. That parent may love their child more than anything in the universe, but the kid isn't going to experience it that way because the parent didn't take the time to build a relationship with them.

Similarly, in the professional world you can't just attend a few networking events and then expect you can call in favors and get help when you need it the way you could if you had a real relationship with those people. The people in business who can call in a favor or ask a co-worker for help can do so because they have helped the other person in the past and they have a good, strong relationship with them.

It takes some time to build up connections with others. There is no quick way to do it. But if you take the time to genuinely get to know people and help them. They will be willing to come to your aid when you need it. And they will also be willing to do what you ask them.

Influence

Having someone else do what you want them to is what influence is all about. Those who lead others—CEOs, managers, teachers, nurses, doctors, parents, politicians, and spiritual or religious leaders—all have the same thing in common.

They need to get other people to do what they want them to.

Sometimes this is for the person's own good, as in the case of a teacher, nurse, or religious leader. Sometimes this is for the good of the company, as in the case of the CEO or manager. Sometimes this is for the good of the nation or the world, in the case of a politician.

But no matter what the motivation, influence is about convincing people that they want to do what you want them to do.

It is important to note what influence is not. It is not coercion. It is not *forcing* people to do what you want, either in a nice way—carrot—or a bad way—stick. It is not manipulating people. It is not tricking people into doing what you want them to.

In all ways, influence is about persuading people, to see things your way. Then they make the decision to do what you want them to of their own free will. This is always better than using punishments and rewards, or manipulating or tricking people. Obviously.

So, how do you develop the skill of influence? Well, the first thing you need to do is stop using the carrot or the stick. And stop trying to manipulate or trick people into doing what you want them to. Once you've cut out those inefficient and morally questionable behaviors, you can start over with more ethical and efficacious methods.

As noted previously, this is not something that you achieve overnight. But start today and you'll be in a much better position to influence people in a year than you could ever imagine at this moment.

Or perhaps you've never had to influence people before but you're starting a new job or expecting a new baby and you want to get things right from the beginning.

Start by building trust and a strong relationship. This means explaining. A lot. The other person needs to know *why* you want them to do something.

So instead of just giving an order to an employee, take a few moments to talk with them, ask them about their life and actually care about their answers, and then explain why you need them to do this task. They need to understand how what they're doing is important. And that how well they do this one task affects the whole company. With this higher level knowledge in mind, the person can go at their task—even if it might not be the most interesting job—with more willingness and motivation because they understand that it's important.

The same goes for dealing with children or others whose behaviour you're trying to influence for their own good. Not many people are going to argue that for a child to be healthy and happy, they need to get enough sleep. It has been proven scientifically and there are good reasons why sleep is important. And yet, this continues to be a battle in many homes.

But it doesn't have to be.

As a parent, from the time a child is small you can explain why sleep is important. You can remind them that their brain needs its nightly bath. There is a detox that happens every nighttime in the brain, which is why if you stay up too late you feel horrible and like your brain isn't working. It's because if you are awake, then your brain can't have its bath.

You can also tell the child about how if they don't get

enough sleep and something annoying happens, they won't have the brainpower to deal with it. It's well known that without enough sleep it is not possible for us to deal with stress. We don't have what's needed without having got enough sleep the night before.

And of course, mentioning to them that they get smarter, taller, and healthier when they sleep is always a big seller. The brain makes connections and puts things in long-term memory when we sleep, thus making the child smarter. The body grows and heals itself mostly during rest.

When a child has it explained in this way and understands the benefits of going to sleep, they are much more likely to be cooperative.

That's what influence is all about.
1. Build strong relationships.
2. Explain your way of thinking.
3. Have them consider your way of thinking.
4. Ask them to do what you want them to do.

You won't always get a resounding yes. And sometimes the people still won't co-operate. It may take some time to repair relationships or build-up non-existent ones.

But once these issues have been attended to, you are much more likely to get people to do what you want—and feel good about it—if you use influence.

So, start building healthy relationships today. And try explaining and asking when you want someone to do something. You may be surprised at the results.

PRACTICING EMOTIONAL INTELLIGENCE

What does Emotional Intelligence look like in real life?

So we've learned in more detail what the four Rs are and the skills that go with them, what does EI actually look like in real life? Now that you've improved your emotional intelligence, you may wonder what sort of actions will start showing up in your behavior. The following chapter is going to give you a picture of what emotional intelligence will look like in your daily life.

Considering Emotions: Your Own and Others

As you begin developing your Emotional Intelligence, you will notice emotions more in general and you will pay more attention to them, thus saving yourself and others from a lot of pain and improving your life because you'll be making better decisions based on having a more complete picture of what's going on.

Manage Your Feelings

Once you practice observing your emotions in your Feelings Pot, you will be able to release them more quickly. And you'll also be able to replace them with more positive emotions that will help you accomplish your goals and feel better about your life in general.

Respond Instead of React

If you can learn this, it is going to be the most powerful thing you can use to build strong relationships and improve your life. Responding instead of reacting means taking a pause between something happening and you taking some sort of action.

When you react, there is no space between what happens and your reaction to it. A driver honks at you, you're instantly angry. Your girlfriend forgets your birthday, you're instantly hurt. Most times these instant reactions cause pain either for us or for others because we don't think about the consequences, we just react.

But if you can just have a tiny space after something happens to hold those emotions in your Feelings Pot and not do or say anything until you have even a small amount of control over your feelings, then you will have a chance to make better decisions.

You can Take and Give Feedback

Feedback is often referred to as criticism—or sometimes constructive criticism. And, let's face it; most people are not good at giving or receiving feedback.

When giving, we are often too harsh and only focus on giving feedback on what's not working. Then if we receive the same kind of feedback on our work, or ourselves we almost always take it personally.

It's as if someone has punched you in the gut when someone tells you your work isn't perfect. And it's weird because of course you know that what you've done isn't perfect. Usually, that's why you've requested feedback—because you want to make it better. But it still hurts.

As you become more emotionally intelligent, you will be able to give and receive feedback better. When you give feedback, you will be conscious of others' emotions and so you will tell the truth but give feedback on what's working, as well as what they could do to make it even better.

Also, as feedback is offered to you, you will be able to hold whatever feelings you have about it in your pot and give yourself some space to allow those emotions. Once the feeling has subsided through you paying attention to it, then you can take the straight facts and make things better. Without debilitating feelings holding you back, you will make use of that feedback in order to improve whatever it is you're trying to make better, thus improving your whole life in the process.

Be Authentic, Empathetic, and Helpful

As you pay more attention to your feelings and those of others, you may find that all the roles you've been playing start to drop away. For example, you might be the strong type or the cheerful type or the brooding type. But now that you are in touch with how you are feeling, you may find it more difficult to play a part. Because you will know how you are feeling—instead of burying the emotions—and you may want to express how you feel. This may not jive with who others think you are. But they will get used to the new, authentic you. And they will probably like you better for it.

Being emotionally intelligent means considering others feelings as well as your own. By doing this, you will understand others and be more concerned about their welfare. This translates into increased empathy for other people. And if you understand and have empathy for others you will naturally want to help them and make their lives easier.

A by-product of emotional intelligence is that it will

make you into a kinder, more real person. You will have more concern for other people and you will be helpful without any effort. It will just be your default mode, as an emotionally intelligent human being.

Keep Your Word

This is similar to the previous section. If you are considering other people and how they feel, you will automatically not want to let them down. You will likely find yourself considering whether you should give your word that you will do something. You will be more careful about what responsibilities you accept. And when you decide to do something for someone else, you'll definitely keep your word more. And if you can't keep it, you'll let the other person know what happened as early as possible, you'll apologize, and you'll try to make it right in any way possible.

Protect Yourself from Other People's Emotions

The downside of all this talk of emotional intelligence is that some people are using it to further their own gains. They are using it to manipulate others.

The good thing is that you will be far more alert than most people and if someone is trying to manipulate you, you will be more likely to pick up on it than the average person.

As an emotionally intelligent person, you'll pick up on

the body language that suggests that something is not quite right in what they're saying. You'll hear it in their tone of voice. You'll ask questions that may put them on the spot and reveal what their true intentions are. And so, you can protect yourself from those who may wish to prey on your emotions for their own selfish gains.

Armed with your EI, you may also protect others from such emotional predators and prevent them from being harmed.

How can Emotional Intelligence Improve My Relationships?

EI can improve both personal and professional relationships. Read on for practical suggestions on how to use emotional intelligence at home and at work.

Your Relationship with Yourself

Many people in the world today are unhappy. You may be one of them. Or even if you don't consider yourself particularly miserable, you may have times when you feel upset, sad, or confused. Using Emotional Intelligence can help you have a happier more peaceful internal state.

When negative emotions come up, your job is not to

get lost in them or get down on yourself for having them. Just hold them in your Feelings Pot and pay attention to them without thinking about them. As the feeling subsides, you will feel better.

Being able to manage your emotions will make your life so much better in so many ways. People who are unhappy are the ones in the world that are lashing out and making others unhappy. If you are at peace and can manage negative emotions when they arise, then you will be the one who is spreading peace in the world.

This is what Gandhi meant when he said... "Be the change you want to see in the world." It is not about external changes but about changing your internal world.

Try this technique.

Keep a Journal

This is a habit that many high achievers do as part of their daily routine. If you would like to increase your self-awareness, consider writing in a journal every day for a few minutes before bed. This can be a good way of getting the unresolved emotional baggage out and may even help you fall asleep easier because you've dumped the garbage from your mind.

When you write in your journal, you can record events, but also write how you felt about what happened. This can help you process your emotions and be better able to recognize them. As you proceed, make sure you are completely honest with yourself and how you felt.

Question Your Own Opinions

When you find yourself arguing with another person or even with a news event or something you read on the internet, try to take a breath and question why you think that. There are other people who think differently and they are actually not wrong - even if they don't agree with you.

This can be very difficult with people who believe they are always right. If you are one of these people, try saying... Well, I know that I'm right but I wonder why they think the way that they do? Or ask... If I had their background and their worldview, how would I see this situation?

For many people this may be stretching muscles that they've never used before but the more you practice, the more you will develop an open mind, which is key to both emotional intelligence and being a fully mature member of a democratic civilization.

Friendships

EI will help you be a better friend. You'll be able to empathize and be more helpful to your friends when they are in difficult situations. One of the best things you can try with a friend is the old adage to walk a mile in their shoes. Sometimes we secretly judge our friends for what seem to be silly decisions that they ought to know not to make. There are times when our advice can come off as slightly critical. To avoid this, use the Walk a Mile technique (see below).

Also, one thing not to do in friendships or any other relationship is dwell on the past. People with high EI tend to leave the past behind and not dredge it up again. This can be something you can practice as well. When your friend says... Yeah, but remember that time you left me standing in the rain, while you went to the party without me? Or whatever it might be. Don't be tempted to come up with your own. Be the bigger person and just say... Yes, I was pretty inconsiderate back then. But I'm trying to be better now.

Try this technique.

Walk a Mile in Someone Else's Shoes

When your friend tells you about some decision that has now led to a difficult situation, instead of letting your mind jump into judging mode, take a couple seconds to imagine things from a different point of view.

Actually imagine things from your friend's eyes. You have your friend's background, family, job and life situation. What would you have done if you were your friend? You probably would have made the exact same choice. Or maybe not. But this will give you a more empathetic view of the situation and can help you to be more understanding of your friend's difficulties, which will make you a better friend.

Family Relationships

You can use emotional intelligence to help you improve relationships with family members and friends. EI will help you notice sooner when they are upset. It will allow you to anticipate when something you are planning to do might upset them and will help you explain it to them in a way that they can hear.

Using EI with your children will help you be more sensitive to their situation. Hopefully you will consider using influence more and punishments and rewards less.

If you have been using punishments and rewards with your children for a long time, it may take some time for them to get used to this different sort of relationship. You may need to build up their trust in this new way of doing things.

Start by explaining exactly what you're doing. That you want to be more sensitive to how they feel and that you want to try explaining more and ordering less.

In most cases, your children will be happy about this change and will feel that you are keeping them in the loop and explaining why they need to do what you want them to do. Because of this, they may be more likely to want to do what you want them to do.

Of course, there are always kids whose personalities will still want to stir things up or who may take some time coming around to this new way of doing things. It's important that you have patience and continue to use your empathy skills to see things from their point of view. In most cases, the children will be glad to move into this more open, transparent, and authentic relationship with you. Just make sure you explain so that they aren't completely taken off guard by the changes you are trying to make.

Try this technique.

Two Stars and a Wish

When you are giving a family member feedback, use the Two Stars and a Wish method to be encouraging, straightforward, and to help them improve without endangering your relationship.

Two Stars and a Wish reminds you to look for strengths as well as weaknesses. When you are giving feedback, communicate something that the person has done well, then tell them what needs to be changed and improved, and lastly leave them on a positive note by indicating another positive thing that they've done.

Example

I loved supper tonight, honey. Next time, could you just put in a little less Cayenne pepper? Maybe we could put the shaker on the table for those who want to add more? Thanks so much for making it. It was great to come home and have it ready for us to eat.

Star: I loved supper.

Wish: Next time a little less cayenne pepper.

Star: Thanks for making supper, it was so nice to come home and it was ready.

The first compliment sets the person up to be open to hearing what you have to say. The request is in terms of how to improve, not what was wrong and is the way that is the least likely to hurt someone's feelings. The thanks at the end, reiterates that you appreciated what the other person did and encourages them to want to keep doing it.

Intimate Relationships

Emotional intelligence will probably make the most difference in your intimate relationship with your partner. Many misunderstandings and arguments could be prevented if you had been using EI.

Now that you are familiar with the ways you can pay attention to what is going on inside of you and how you can infer what is happening inside your partner—and then confirm with them, of course—you will be able to avoid many problems that would have previously become big fights.

The first time you use EI with your partner, you may be speaking and acting in your usual way and then suddenly you will wake up and take a step back. You'll put your emotion in the Feelings Pot and breathe. Then you may choose a different way of responding than usual. Your partner may be confused that you're not playing your part properly in the play that the two of you have been acting out for years.

But as you continue to try to understand both your own and the other person's feelings, you will find that your partner is quite happy about how the usual fight has turned into an amicably resolved discussion.

Your relationship may not be as exciting with the big ups and downs and drama. But it will definitely be more peaceful and happy when you use emotional intelligence to navigate any difficult patches you and your partner may encounter.

Try this technique.

What Can I Learn?

When your partner criticizes you in some way,

instead of becoming defensive and saying that you didn't do it, or you did do it, or you meant to do it, etc. practice stripping away the insults and emotional baggage that accompanies the message and asking what you can learn from the words.

Example
I can't believe you didn't take the garbage out. That is so irresponsible of you. I can't stand it when it smells like that. How did I stay married to someone like you for this long?

There are a lot of other messages in those sentences. But what can you truly take away that could be useful? If you can separate all the personal judgments, you might be able to learn something.

1. Original: I can't believe you didn't take the garbage out.

What you could learn: Your spouse considers it your job to take the garbage out.

Response: You could just consider it your job to take out the garbage and do it. Or you could discuss how to equitably split the job so that you both do equal amounts of work.

2. Original: That is so irresponsible of you.

What you could learn: Well, in this case you need to consider whether this is true or not. If it's not true, you can safely ignore it. If it is true, then maybe you can learn something about yourself, such as you need reminders in order to fulfill your responsibilities.

Response: Ignore it if it's not actually true but just your partner's emotional response when they're upset with you. Or if it is true, then maybe you will set a reminder on your phone. Or ask your partner to simply leave a note that says, garbage, if you forget.

3. *Original:* I can't stand it when it smells like that.

What you could learn: It bothers your partner when the garbage isn't taken out and it starts to smell.

Response: You can make your partner happier by just doing this one small task.

4. *Original:* How did I stay married to someone like you for this long?

What you could learn: Your partner is frustrated with your behaviour in not taking the garbage out. Do you also shirk other household responsibilities?

Response: Maybe you and your partner need to sit down and hammer out exactly who does what and decide on a system that both of you can agree on. Maybe you need to hire a housekeeper, so that neither of you has to do it. Or maybe you need to stop shirking and start doing what you've been neglecting.

This is not easy. But if you can do it, it will remove a lot of conflict from your relationship.

Professional Relationships

At work is where your knowledge of Emotional Intelligence could really change whether you are successful or not. You have no idea how your feelings have sabotaged things for you in the workplace in the past.

That time you ignored your co-worker when they were upset, came back to haunt you when you needed their help. You blamed it on them not being a good person, but really, it was your own karma coming back around to kick you in the pants.

That time you were passed over for a promotion? While you thought it was because your co-worker had more training than you, it was really because your boss didn't want to deal with the drama you always seem to bring along with you in the workplace.

And the reason your employees are unmotivated and always behind is because they feel that you only see them as cogs in a machine and not people. Treating them with kindness and compassion, while still leading well and not letting them walk all over you, will make a big difference in the bottom line for your department.

But all that is in the past now, because you're going to be building authentic relationships and connections with others at work because you can't help it now that you know about Emotional Intelligence. As these relationships get stronger, you may see your success in the workplace going up because you are better at influencing people.

It is a myth that business isn't personal. *Everything* is personal, no matter what business books will tell you. And the sooner you can tap into the power of personal connections for the good of yourself and those around you, the sooner you will find success and achievement at work.

Try these techniques at work.

Watch Your Words

One of the things that people could do to improve their relationships at work is to pay more attention to the words they use. Words have power. Though we need to also think about *how* we are saying things, in terms of our non-verbal communication, it is also important to think about what we are saying. There is more than one way of saying the same thing. And often people will be able to hear what you're saying - or not hear it, depending on the words you use.

For example, there are ways of saying something that will make your listener angry. They will shut down and not be able to hear what you are trying to tell them. Of course, there are other ways of saying the exact same thing. If you speak with empathy, then you are much more likely to have the person open, listening, and able to hear what you'd like to communicate.

Obviously, the second way of communicating is better if you want to actually have people listen to you. And if you want to have influence with them eventually, then they need to listen to you and consider what you have to say.

Let's look at how you can say things in different ways and how that affects the results you get from other people.

Example

"This is a filthy mess. How can you work like this? Only a pig would keep a workspace like this one."

"Your workspace needs to be cleaned up and I would appreciate it if you kept it cleaner going forward. By when can you have it tidied?"

In the first example, all the sentences are just criticisms and rhetorical questions that hurt the person, maybe make them not want to clean up (but instead go curl up in a hole and cry), and turn them against the person speaking to them in this way.

In the second example, the problem is stated clearly and without criticism or negative emotions. The question asked is useful in that it requires the person to assess how long it will take them to clean up and then gives them a deadline. This way of speaking to another person doesn't turn a situation into a problem. And the person is more likely have a good relationship with the person they're asking to clean up. The person who is doing the cleaning may even make more of an effort because they were spoken to respectfully, and the relationship was maintained. This will make it far more likely that they will want to do what the person is asking them.

Manage Emotions so You can Speak Your Truth

One of the problems with feelings is that they get us so mixed up and turned around that we don't know which way is up and we are unable to see things clearly. When your temper is high, you will not see other people or situations reasonably. You'll see everything skewed by your emotions. And if you speak in this state, you are far more likely to say hurtful things that you realize later you didn't really mean.

Using EI to manage your emotions and bring yourself back to an even keel will allow you to speak your truth when you communicate, instead of letting your feelings express themselves.

Usually your feelings are only concerned with

spewing themselves everywhere and have no worry about the problems they will cause you in your life. If you are angry about something, it would be better for you to hold that feeling in the pot and pay attention to it until it subsides. Then you can look at the issue reasonably and from a calm perspective. You can choose your words so that they don't hurt others. You can make a rational decision.

Some of the reasons that you were angry may come into play when you choose what to do. But you will not be run by your emotions and you will, instead, use them as tools.

Remember The Feeling Three from the beginning of the book: Emotions make good tools but bad bosses. Use them properly but don't let them use you. Or you will find that they cause you more trouble than good in your relationships.

To manage stress, try splashing cold water on your face and getting some fresh air. This helps to reduce anxiety and will reset your mind so that you can come at whatever you are facing with a fresh perspective. Also, if you are anxious, try to avoid caffeine, as this will exacerbate your anxiety.

To manage heavier emotions, such as fear, try intense aerobic exercise. This tends to move your energy and provide a pick me up that will allow you to more properly manage what you are going through.

Reduce Fear of Rejection by Keeping Your Sense of Self Out of it

When you have something important like a presentation or where you have to offer ideas to a group and you're worried that you might be rejected, try to keep your sense of self out of it. You don't want to be too emotionally invested in whatever it is because then if you're rejected it can be intensely painful.

For example, if you're giving a presentation that is then criticized, you can keep your ego from taking a beating, by just keeping your sense of self out of it. How do you do this?

Try this detaching technique.

Detach

As you are creating the presentation and especially before you speak to the group, imagine that there are emotional ties between you and the presentation - visualize strings attaching you to the project and feel those emotions. Then imagine taking a big pair of scissors and cutting those strings. Sense that feeling of being invested in your idea fade or disappear.

You can also pretend that it's not your idea that you're just presenting it for someone else. If that was the case, then you probably wouldn't care much if it was criticized because you were just the messenger, so to speak.

Respond Without Reacting to the Emotions Coming at You

Often what causes the most difficulties in relationships is that we get caught up in someone else's emotions. Those mirror neurons that were mentioned earlier come into play and if the other person is angry, then we get angry. If the other person is sad and disappointed, then so are we. It is a recipe for disaster.

Everyone has probably had the experience of walking into a room calmly and feeling at peace, having someone you know attack you, and being instantly angry. An argument follows that undermines the relationship and can lead to more trouble down the road.

But what if you could walk into the room, feel the anger coming at you, and instead of being pulled into that energy field, taking a breath. While you breathe, you put the anger you feel in the pot and watch it. You realized that actually it's not your anger. It's the other person's. You release it and then ask the person to tell you what's wrong.

If your emotions are calm, then the mirror neurons will once more go to work, helping the other person find some peace so that the problem can be discussed properly without emotions distracting you both from finding a solution.

This is the difference between reacting and responding.

At first, you may find it difficult, but you can use the exercise of taking three conscious breaths before you speak or counting to ten, either of which may give you enough time to watch your feelings and respond instead of react.

Sometimes the emotions may be too strong and you may need to have them in the pot longer in order for you to release them. If that's the case, you need to politely ask to speak about the issue a little later when you're calmer. If you can, then remove yourself from the person making you angry and go somewhere alone so that you can observe your feelings until they dissipate.

At that point, you can reinitiate the discussion with the purpose of working together to find a solution. If the other person wants to express how they feel, that's fine as long as it doesn't turn into another argument. You will have to remain calm and keep watching each emotion that comes up as you put it into the Feelings Pot.

This is not easy and will take some practice to have enough Emotional Intelligence to be able to do this successfully.

Try this technique.

<u>It Must Not be Easy...</u>

This is a very simple strategy where you just make a small effort to imagine things from the other person's perspective. This works great with a difficulty with your boss or with people who work under you. What you do is say to yourself...

It must not be easy... and then fill in the blank.

Examples

It must not be easy to be a new principal and have all those unfamiliar responsibilities.

It must not be easy to be a worker who has been in their job so long and is worried about losing it because they are getting too old and their knowledge is becoming irrelevant.

It must not be easy to keep picking boyfriends who belittle you.

It must not be easy when you have low self-esteem

to even think about getting a better job or asking for a raise.

TROUBLESHOOTING EMOTIONAL INTELLIGENCE

The following sections discuss problems that may come up as your try to put EI into practice in your life. By preparing yourself for some of these common issues, you won't be surprised by them. And you will know what to do if these roadblocks pop up.

Who are You Without Your Problems?

An issue that may come up when you start using Emotional Intelligence is that you may wonder who you are without your problems. If I'm not the person with marital troubles or that can't get that promotion at work, then who am I? You may feel a bit lost when some of your problems start disappearing and you may feel uncomfortable with your successes. It may seem strange but it is actually quite common. It's where the whole imposter syndrome comes from where people don't feel that they deserve the success and accolades that they've achieved.

But if this happens, it is handled the same way any other emotion is. Put the discomfort in your Feelings Pot and observe it until it dissipates. When you are free of the feeling, then you may begin to see your success from a different perspective.

Internal Conflict: When Emotions Continue to Overwhelm You

It is quite likely at the beginning that your feelings will continue to get the better of you and overwhelm your attempts to manage them. That's fine. Just tell yourself that it is as it is. Then try again. Sometimes your Feelings Pot will get quite full because you have so many emotions coming at you. This is also fine.

At first, you may only notice them once they're over. That's the beginning of your awareness practice. Then you will suddenly awaken when you're in the middle of the emotion. And you may not be able to stop yourself from playing out the scenario that you've already set in motion. But eventually you'll be able to notice the feeling *before* it comes to full strength. And at that point, that's when you are truly starting to manage your emotions.

Sometimes you will not be able to control your mind when you're in the grip of a strong emotion. Even if you try, you will not be able to stop that feedback loop, where your mind keeps feeding the feeling with thoughts about what it thinks caused it.

That's okay. When that happens, do anything you can think of to change your state. Once you've gotten a little distance from the feeling, you may be able to bring up the memory and the emotion will pop up again so that you can put it in your Feelings Pot and observe it. At that point, it will be weaker and you should be able to handle it.

When your emotions are overwhelming, anything that can bring you back to the present moment is useful—listening to or playing music, going for a walk or exercising, getting out in nature, watching a movie or TV, or if you know how to meditate you could try that as well. Once you're present in the moment, that will help you manage your emotions.

Losing Control of Your Emotions/Behaviour

At the beginning, you will still lose control of your behavior when you're in the grip of strong emotions. There are old patterns that are not that easy to get rid of and when they come up in certain situations, you may have an instant emotional reaction that you can't control.

The most important thing is not to attack others when you are in the power of these feelings. This almost always ends badly with you saying or doing things that you regret.

Instead, when you feel that you can't control yourself, you need to get away from other people. If you're at work, go to your office or cubicle and request that others not disturb you. If people really won't leave you alone, then go into the bathroom until you're calm enough to make a rational decision.

If you're at home, you should have a space you can go to until you're under control again. Explain to your family and friends that you're trying to be more careful with your words and actions. That when you're very upset, you're going to isolate yourself so that you don't say or do things that you will regret later. Most people will understand.

Once you've isolated yourself, it's important to allow those feelings to be, pay attention to them without thinking and let them subside. There are several techniques you can use, such as counting breaths and paying attention to your senses.

You will feel very miserable while the emotion is in control but as you watch it, the feeling will lose its power and you will start to feel better. That is how you will know whether it's you or the feeling that's in charge. The worse you feel, the more likely the emotion is being the boss. When it becomes a useful tool again, you will feel more peaceful and that is how you know that you are in control again.

Lastly, be gentle with yourself when an emotion does take over. The fact that you realize that it's taken over means that it is not in complete control. Remind yourself that you'll get better at this as you go on. And follow the steps for how to release emotions.

Too Much Empathy

Some people are too hard and lacking sympathy. Those people will benefit from Emotional Intelligence in that they will learn to become more compassionate and empathetic.

But others have the opposite problem. Some people are too empathetic. They become engrossed in the emotions of others and lose themselves when they try to help.

The kinds of problems these people suffer from are the following. They may find themselves being taken advantage of. They may give more than they have and become depleted of energy. They may so lose themselves in someone else that they blindly follow a person who means them or others harm.

It is important for a person who has natural empathy

to protect themselves and create healthy boundaries in their life.

They need to be able to recognize when they are giving too much because that is just as unhealthy as giving too little to others around you.

When you find yourself giving to another person, it's helpful to step back, observe your feelings, and determine whether they are your own or whether you are just picking up on another person's emotions so strongly that you imagine those feelings are your own. If you recognize that you're giving too much, you need to stop immediately. Have a calm conversation with the person. They may not be happy about it, but stand firm. You need to protect yourself—even if it makes the other person unhappy.

If they really care about you, they will not want to continue to take more than you can give. And if they do want to keep taking from you, then they don't actually care about you but only about what they can get out of the relationship.

If you are one of these people and have a hard time telling whether you're giving too much in a relationship, then it's also helpful to have someone that you truly trust to give you their opinion.

Giving more than is right will inevitably make you unhappy and that can also be an indication that the relationship isn't balanced and that you should rethink your part in it.

Not Hanging on to Positive Emotions

Another challenge that doesn't seem like a problem at all is when you experience positive emotions you try to hang on to them. People who do this like to relive happy moments to the point of it becoming excessive. They also want to hang on to people who make them feel happy until sometimes they destroy the relationship that they want to preserve—all because they are holding on so tightly that they end up squeezing all the love out of the situation until there's nothing left.

To avoid this happening to you, now that you are more aware of your emotions, it's important to keep in mind The Feeling Three: Emotions are just passing through.

Even the good ones.

In the same way that you release negative feelings, knowing that they will soon pass away if you hold them, you have to let go of the good ones when it's time for them to go. Part of being able to do this is having faith that you will have more good emotions. Yes, they pass. But they will come again.

If you can believe that you will have good feelings again, that is the first step in letting them go when it's their time to move on.

Expecting Others to be Emotionally Intelligent

It is important to keep in mind as you become more aware of yours and others' feelings that most people do not have much awareness of their emotions. They will not be able to respond. They will likely just react as they have always done.

What you need to remember is that they are at the level that they're at and they can't help it. You may possibly influence them to become more interested in improving their Emotional Intelligence but only offer suggestions if they ask. When communicating with EI, make sure it is *with* it and not *about* it. It is unnecessary to convert others to your way of life.

This challenge can go two ways.

1. You expect others to be emotionally intelligent and are disappointed in them when they're not.
2. You want others to be as emotionally intelligent as you are and try to convince them that they should try it.

Either way, you will likely be annoying to others and will damage your relationships instead of building them up. In both situations, you could come across as holier-than-thou wanting the others to be something they're not and—even if you don't really think that—setting yourself up as an example that they should follow.

The first case is pretty straightforward. You don't want to be a jerk and think you're better than someone else is only because you learned to be more aware. So, be careful that you're not setting yourself up as better than the other person who has less EI.

In the second case, you definitely mean well but there's also something self-serving in wanting to be someone else's savior. There's nothing wrong with sharing something great that's happening in your life. But keep it to that—sharing. Don't expect them to want to have higher EI. And don't try to convince them to join you.

If you really want to be good at Emotional Intelligence, then simply practice it in everyday life. *Be* emotionally intelligent. Connect with others. Use your empathy to help. Build strong relationships.

Be a person who cares about other people.

If someone notices that you're happier, calmer, and more peaceful and then asks you why, you can tell them and since they were looking for the information, then they will likely be more ready to hear it. If you go around handing out advice to people who aren't ready, you're just going to end up in a conversation that will likely involve strong feelings and that will not help you or them.

The important thing is that you are getting better at using your Emotional Intelligence. Others can follow your path or not, it doesn't matter. What matters is that you respond instead of react and that you know that the quality of *your* life is improving.

Dealing with Criticism

This is one of the most difficult things that any person can face. When someone criticizes us, we often feel like we've been emotionally kicked in the stomach. It's surprising. It hurts. And we often don't know what we should do about it. But before we do anything, we might want to try practicing the following technique, which can give us more emotional freedom when it comes to criticism and may give us the distance we need to respond instead of having a knee jerk emotional reaction.

Be the Force Field

Everyone has seen how a force field works on a sci fi show. Someone tosses a rock at it and the force field absorbs it. The rock doesn't bounce off and hit the person who threw it. Likewise, you can have a protective force field around you, so that when someone criticizes you, your force field can absorb it.

This protects you from emotional hurt. It can also improve your relationships because you will not be getting into unnecessary conflict with others.

Example

Why can't you call me when you get home? You're so self-centered and thoughtless.

Usual response: I am not. Sometimes I remember to call. But last night when I got home, the light wasn't on, so I couldn't see to put my key in the lock and I got so upset about that. When I got in, I had to talk to my roommate about leaving the light on and then we kind of got in a fight. And when we stopped fighting, I was so stressed out that I had to have a bath. Then I was sleepy and I went straight to bed, forgetting to call you.

EI being the force field response:

You're right. Sometimes I don't think of other people. I'm sorry I forgot. There were circumstances but that's no excuse. Next time, I'll set a reminder so that I won't forget to call you.

With the first response, it's highly likely that you will continue to argue because you're both defending yourselves and your viewpoint. When you allow the force field to absorb the stone and agree with and apologize for your behaviour, usually the person is taken aback and stops attacking you. When they

110

push and you push back, then the fight keeps going. But when they push and you just take it, you've absorbed their negative energy with your force field, so that it doesn't hurt you or them.

The only thing to be careful of is that you don't take what they're saying to heart and get hurt by their words. With this technique, you shouldn't take what they're saying personally but you do admit your part in things and apologize.

IN CONCLUSION: ENHANCE YOUR LIFE WITH EMOTIONAL INTELLIGENCE

Enhancing Your Life with Emotional Intelligence

Now that you have read this book, you have a lot more awareness of your emotions than when you started. You understand that emotions aren't the bad guys, that they're fleeting, that they make good tools but bad bosses.

You've learned to recognize your own feelings, manage them, and if necessary replace them with more helpful emotions. You also have more skills for picking up on how others are feeling. And you can now use all of that information to connect with other people and build stronger relationships. Then if you need to influence those same people, you have a much better chance of them actually listening to you.

You've also seen what Emotional Intelligence looks like in real life, how it can improve your relationships and communication with others. And we've even had a glance at where you might get tripped up and made suggestions for what you can do to avoid the troubles and pitfalls that some people fall into when they begin using Emotional Intelligence.

Connecting with People and Deepening Relationships

The most important way that Emotional Intelligence can improve your life is that it will help you to have healthy, strong relationships with the people that you care about at home and at work.

This is what life is all about when you get right down to it. Most people at the end of their life don't regret what happened in their career but what happened or didn't happen in their personal lives.

Don't make that mistake.

Yes, EI can help you be more successful in all areas of your life, including work. But it's most important contribution to your life will be in leading a happier life with deep, strong relationships with your loved ones and friends.

If you only use EI for this, you will have fulfilled the mission of this book. But that's not the only thing that will get better when you begin incorporating EI into your life on a daily basis and for the long term.

Making Better Decisions

You have a lot of information that you've learned about Emotional Intelligence but it won't do you any good if you keep it up there in your head. You need to bring EI into your heart and into your life. You need to use that information in your day-to-day choices. There are a few ways you can make better decisions using EI.

The first way you'll make better decisions using EI is by understanding other people better. This will keep you from making mistakes in conversations and allow you to help others more easily because you'll naturally be more tuned into them.

The second way, you can improve your decision-making capabilities is by paying attention to your own feelings and the emotions of others around you. This gives you more information in order to make a better decision. You might call this listening to your gut or maybe intuition. But either way, you'll be tapping into a power that has more information than your brain alone.

The third way that EI can improve how you make your choices is by helping you to clear out emotions that are blocking you from making good decisions.

Sometimes we have old reactions that are holding us back. We just can't make good decisions when it comes to money, or our career, or our love life. But if you use EI and hold those emotions that come up, it can allow you to release the past's hold on *you.* Releasing those old emotions can set you free from those automated reactions and will allow you to make another choice that will improve your life and let you have success in those areas where you never have been able to succeed before.

Or in other cases, we have a strong emotional reaction that we can't let go of and that prevents us from making a good choice. By using your EI skills, you will free yourself from these Bad Boss emotions and turn them back into the useful tools that they can be if handled correctly.

Living a More Positive Life

Emotional Intelligence will help you release negative emotions and encourage positive feelings. This will help you to feel better about yourself and your life, even if nothing changes on the outside.

Internally, you will have cleaned things up and that will make you feel more happy and peaceful.

But on the outside you will be able to handle when things don't go right, which happens a lot if we're being honest. You will be able to better understand other people and what motivates them to behave the way they do. This will help you to connect with them on a deeper level and if you take the time to build strong relationships with them, then you will also be able to influence them to want to do what you want them to do.

This could lead to more success in your personal and professional life. But even if by some chance it doesn't, you'll still be a much happier person if you can manage your emotions and release the negative ones.

Emotional Intelligence gives you a bit of a superpower because you will have insight that will elude others. And, of course, like all great super heroes, you need to use this power wisely and always for the good of all involved.

Next Steps

1. Start noticing your emotions. Link this practice to a habit you already have. Leave yourself notes. Do whatever it takes to simply pay more attention to how you feel.
2. Try holding the emotions you feel in your Feelings Pot. Allow them to be. Take a breath and let the feeling dissipate.
3. Once you've become adept at noticing and managing your own emotions, pay closer attention to others and see what you can

become aware of.

4. Be sure and confirm your observations, so that they are not simply assumptions, which can get you into trouble sometimes.

5. Then engage with others, use empathy, and connect and deepen the relationship.

6. When you feel that you have a strong relationship, attempt to influence someone by explaining your side of things. Tell them why you want them to do what you want them to do. Then *ask* them to do it. You may be surprised at how eager people are to help someone they truly respect and care about.

7. Watch out for some of those challenges that may come up and if you meet any of them, refer back to this book for how to deal with them.

You now have the knowledge, skills, and abilities to become more Emotionally Intelligent. Your part now is to go out there and practice. Get good at knowing yourself and others. And build those relationships. You will be happier and you'll find more success in life if you do.

Good luck.

YOUR OPINION IS IMPORTANT

First of all, thank you for purchasing this book. I know you could have picked any number of books to read, but you picked this book and for that I am extremely grateful.

If you enjoyed this book and found some benefit in reading this, I'd like to hear from you and hope that you could take some time to post a review on Amazon. Your feedback really makes a difference to me.

If you'd like to leave a review all you need to do is to go to the book's product page on Amazon and click on ***"Write a Customer Review"***

I wish you all the best for your journey!

ABOUT THE AUTHOR

 Diane always considered herself an introvert, but constantly strived to break out of her shy exterior. As she grew older, she put her mind to learning how to thrive as an introvert in an extrovert world, so she could tackle her shyness and no longer fear the social situations she had grown accustomed to avoiding. This took her on a journey of studying all there was to know about communication and how it affects our everyday lives.

After completing her course in Communication and Media Studies, she embarked on a career as a public relations specialist in a Fortune 500 company. Now, although still an introvert, she no longer fears the social encounters that once held her back from living her life to the full. In fact, she now actually looks forward to them.

Today, she wants to share her journey to social freedom so that other people can learn to blossom in a world full of extroverts. Her desire to teach people how to become better communicators led her to write two books; an ultimate guide to mastering emotional intelligence, and an instruction manual on how to conquer small talk and become an expert conversationalist.

In her free time, she still enjoys learning everything there is to know about language and communication, but also always enjoys spending time with her family and being outdoors.

Learn more about Diane Weston here:
amazon.com/author/dianeweston

BIBLIOGRAPHY

Brackett, M., Rivers, S., & Salovey, P. (2011). Emotional intelligence: Implications for personal, social, academic, and workplace success. *Social and Personality Psychology Compass*

Goleman, D. (1998). Emotional Intelligence: Why It Can Matter More Than IQ

Goleman, D. (2000): Working with Emotional Intelligence

Mayer, J., Salovey, P., & Caruso, D. (2008): Emotional intelligence: New ability or eclectic traits?

Mayer, J. D., Salovey, P., & Caruso, D. R. (2004). Emotional intelligence: Theory, findings, and implications. Psychological Inquiry

Mayer, J. D., Salovey, P., Caruso, D. R., & Sitarenios, G. (2003). Measuring emotional intelligence with the MSCEIT

Petrides, K., Pérez-Gonzalez, J., & Furnham, A. (2007). On the criterion and incremental validity of trait emotional intelligence.

Sarkis, S. (2011). Retrieved from https://www.psychologytoday.com/intl/blog/here-there-and-everywhere/201111/three-recent-studies-emotional-intelligence-ei

Tarko, V. (2006, November 1). Retrieved from https://news.softpedia.com/news/How-Do-Mirror-Neurons-Work-39171.shtml

Printed in Great Britain
by Amazon